Spugete Mystery

By Joy Cowley

Illustrated by Shane Marsh

Dominie Press, Inc.

Publisher: Christine Yuen
Editor: John S. F. Graham
Designer: Lois Stanfield
Illustrator: Shane Marsh

Published by:

꙰ Dominie Press, Inc.

1949 Kellogg Avenue
Carlsbad, California 92008 USA

www.dominie.com

Paperback ISBN 0-7685-1086-4
Library Bound Edition ISBN 0-7685-1535-1
Printed in Singapore by PH Productions Pte Ltd
1 2 3 4 5 6 PH 04 03 02

Table of Contents

Chapter One

Winning Can Be Lonely

Tad couldn't wait for the results of the spelling test. His friend Clarene was top of the class in most subjects, but not spelling. No, sir! Her spelling was terrible. She even spelled *spaghetti*, *spugete*, which was why Tad sometimes called her *Spugete* when he was annoyed with her.

Clarene was pleased. "I love being called *spaghetti*," she said. "It must be my Italian blood."

"You're African-American," Tad said.

"My grandmother was half-Italian," she replied. "That makes me one-eighth Italian, and I just love spaghetti, macaroni, spumoni, panettone..." She went on naming foods Tad had never heard of.

"I'm one-third Italian," Tad said. "And one-third Irish, and my father is an award-winning chef."

Clarene laughed. "No one can be one-third anything."

"Why not?" he demanded.

"You work it out," she replied.

Tad did work it out. He was a *quarter* Italian and a *quarter* Irish. So what? The spugete girl might be good at math, but *he* was better at spelling.

He put up his hand as high as it would go.

"Yes, Tad?" said Miss Barr.

"Who won the spelling test?"

"*Won?*" Miss Barr wrinkled her forehead.

"I mean, who got the best grade?"

"Tad doesn't like losing," Clarene said sweetly.

Miss Barr shook her head. "Tad Casey! Clarene LaValle! You two are so competitive! One day, you might discover that it's awfully lonely to be first in everything. In fact, winning can be so lonely that sometimes it feels like losing."

"Yeah, yeah, yeah," thought Tad. He looked at Clarene, who rolled her eyes at him.

"If you must know," said Miss Barr, "I left the spelling test papers at home, and I'll bring them tomorrow. All right, everyone, time for recess."

Petrov Ulanov, who sat next to Tad, frowned as he put his books away. "It was just a test," he said. "It wasn't an election. Who cares who gets best?"

"I do!" said Tad.

Chapter Two
Life Could Be Boring

Clarene and her mother lived in the same building as Tad, his younger brother Paul, and their father.

There were times when Tad thought he would never get away from Clarene. They were neighbors at school and at home. Tad's father and Clarene's mother were friends, and they often had dinner together. Besides that, Clarene, Tad, and Paul ran a detective business in their building. The Spugete Detectives, as Clarene called it.

Tad complained to his father, "She's in my face all day!"

"She probably says the same thing about you," his father replied. Then he added, "It looks to me like you choose to spend time with each other. If you can't get along, why don't you just stop spending time together?"

Tad didn't reply because he didn't know the answer. He and Clarene argued a lot, but he thought life would be boring without her.

She sat with him on the school bus. "Stop frowning," she said. "You'll win the spelling test."

"I'm not thinking about that," he said, which wasn't quite true.

"I'll get top marks for the rainforest project," she said.

Tad looked sideways at her and imitated Miss Barr: "Winning can be so lonely, sometimes it feels like losing."

"Nah!" She nudged him with her elbow. "I've always got you to talk to."

Tad grinned and looked out the window.

"We should talk," Clarene said. "Not about school. About the Spugete Detectives. You and me and Paul, we should have a meeting this afternoon."

"Why?"

"To define our job in the building," she said. "Are we detectives? Or are we just kids who run errands and do chores? Mr. Milano had Paul sweeping out the toolroom. Mrs. Hutchinson on the fifth floor wants us to deliver flyers for her theater group."

Tad shrugged and said, "We get paid."

"That's not the point," she said. "Highly skilled detectives do not do boring chores."

Tad replied, "Your mother's a highly skilled doctor, and she does your laundry."

"That's family stuff. I'm not talking about that. With family, you're supposed to do that kind of thing. I'm talking about business. Are we a detective agency or aren't we?"

Tad shrugged again. "Do you know what real detectives do when they're out of work?"

"What?"

"They deliver theater flyers around town," he said.

Chapter Three
Substitute Teacher

Miss Barr was not at school the next morning. For the first half-hour, there was no teacher in the classroom. The noise grew louder, and some of the kids started flicking balls of paper on the ends of their rulers. After a while, Mrs. Isbister came in and shushed them all. She said she would be filling in for Miss Barr, who was unavoidably detained.

"What does *unavoidably detained* mean?" Diane Baker asked.

"I believe she's indisposed," said Mrs. Isbister, who liked long words.

"*Indisposed?*" said Diane, who preferred shorter ones.

"Ill," said Mrs. Isbister.

A murmur went through the class. Miss Barr was a popular teacher.

"What's wrong with her?" someone asked.

"We don't have that information," said Mrs. Isbister. "Indeed, we have no information at all. It is possible that Miss Barr has been called away on some urgent family matter. The school secretary is still trying to contact her."

"She could be gone for months!" said Petrov.

"I sincerely hope not," said Mrs. Isbister. "That would be of considerable inconvenience."

Clarene raised her eyebrows at Tad, who shrugged. "So much for the spelling test grades," Tad thought.

Mrs. Isbister tapped on the teacher's desk. "This class is displaying disruptive behavior," she said. "Please settle down and take out your math books."

Diane Baker reached into her desk—not for her book, but for some tissues. She was crying.

"Is there something wrong?" Mrs. Isbister asked her.

"Miss Barr might never come back!" Diane sobbed into a handful of pink tissues.

Tad got a sick, tight feeling in his stomach. Diane cried about a lot of things, but what if she were right? What if Miss Barr weren't coming back? What if she were sick or had moved away to another town?

He might never find out the results of the spelling test.

Chapter Four

Miss Barr is Missing

It was the end of the school day, and still no one knew where Miss Barr was.

"Either that," said Clarene, "or no one's telling us."

"We're detectives, aren't we?" said Tad.

Clarene's eyes lit up. She went to the front of the class where Mrs. Isbister was stacking some books. "Excuse me, Mrs. Isbister, but can you give us Miss Barr's phone number?"

"I'm sorry, Clarene, that information is confidential," Mrs. Isbister replied.

"We just want to find out how she is," Tad said.

"I can assure you, Theodore, the school secretary had been trying to call her all day." Mrs. Isbister gave him a small smile. "This is not your concern."

"Like heck it's not," Tad thought. He grabbed Clarene's arm. "Come on," he said. "We'll miss the bus."

On the bus, several boys and girls were talking about Miss Barr's disappearance. How could one of the most popular teachers in the school be missing?

"There must be dozens of Barrs in the phone book," muttered Clarene.

"Forget it, Spugete," said Tad. "Just like Mrs. Isbister said, the school's been trying to call her all day."

Clarene gave him one of her superior looks. "We don't have to call her. If we had her number, we could look in the phone book and find her address. Then we could go to her house," she explained.

That made sense. Tad frowned. "Hey!" he said. "At the beginning of the school year, Miss Barr sent letters home to parents. This was before you came."

"Not just at the beginning of the year," said Clarene. "My mom got one of those letters, too. She was so impressed that a teacher could write like that."

"Miss Barr said something about it being a privilege to teach me," said Tad. "She said she was looking forward to meeting our family, and if there was anything Dad wanted to know…"

"She wrote down her home phone number!" Clarene cried.

"Dad's not exactly Mr. Clean, but he *does* keep school stuff," said Tad.

"Mom's got a filing cabinet this big," said Clarene, stretching her arms.

Tad said, "If we get Miss Barr's phone number, we can get her address."

"That's what I've been telling you," Clarene pointed out. "You know what we can do? We can go around town delivering Mrs. Hutchinson's theater flyers."

Chapter Five

The Bus is Faster

When Paul heard about the plan, he said, "I'm coming, too."

Tad said, "You're not in Miss Barr's class."

Paul was stubborn. "This is Spugete Detectives work, not schoolwork."

"Paul's right," said Clarene.

"It's on Washington Street, miles and miles away on the other side of town," said Tad. "You'll get tired."

"Two miles," said Spugete. "We can take a city bus."

"Whoa!" Tad's father came in, drying his hands on his chef's apron. "What's all this about a bus?" he asked.

Clarene turned to show him her back-pack. "We're delivering Mrs. Hutchinson's flyers."

"Okay," said Tad's father. "You know the rules. Stay together, don't talk to strangers, and be back before dark. It's spicy fish and rice tonight, with lemon soufflé to follow."

Tad had to admit that Clarene was right. If they walked to Miss Barr's house, they wouldn't be home before midnight.

They waited at the bus stop for a long time. It was rush hour. Paul kept watch for the bus.

"Where's the Spugete Detectives note-book?" said Clarene. "We need to make some notes."

Paul came over to give her the notebook and a pencil.

"First," said Clarene, "we look in Miss

Barr's garage. If her car's gone, we know she's away. If it's there..."

"She's sick in her house," said Paul.

"She'd have to be very sick not to answer the phone," Tad said.

"Maybe she's unconscious," said Clarene, writing in the notebook.

"Or dead," said Paul.

Tad didn't say anything. He leaned across and saw that Clarene had written *unconshis*, but he didn't comment. The tight feeling in his stomach had come back.

They got on the bus when it arrived and sat together in the back.

Tad said, "If the car's there and the house is locked..."

"We'll need to call the police," said Clarene.

"Or an ambulance," said Paul.

Chapter Six

Is Someone There?

The bus stopped at Washington Street. Miss Barr lived at number 115. Tad thought they should hurry, but it was Spugete who insisted they put a pamphlet in every mailbox along the way.

"She could be bleeding to death!" Tad said.

But that Miss Spugete just put her hands on her hips. "Listen, Tad Casey, I told your father we were delivering flyers. Are you going to make a liar out of me? We'll get to Miss Barr's a lot faster if you help."

"Yeah?" Tad said as he grabbed a handful

of flyers. "Who said that detectives didn't deliver theater flyers?"

"And who said they did?" asked Spugete.

Paul sighed, and his shoulders drooped. "I get sick of you two arguing all the time," he groaned.

Miss Barr's house was an odd shape: tall, but not wide, almost like a tower or a lighthouse. It sat by itself on a big lawn, and down by the gate was the garage. The mailbox, near the gate, was stuffed with letters, and there were two newspapers in the driveway. The three detectives looked at the mailbox and then at each other.

Paul said, "If she left, she didn't stop her mail."

Tad walked over to the garage. He tried to see through a small gap in the door, then he went to the side window. "The car's in there," he said.

Clarene and Paul came up behind him and looked over his shoulder. They stood for a long time, staring at the familiar green car.

"Do you think a neighbor would know?" Tad said at last.

"Know what?" asked Paul.

Clarene took a deep breath, which came out again as a sigh. "Let's look at the house," she said.

There was a wicker chair on the front porch and some red flowers on a small plant in a pot. The door had little panes of glass in it. They could see through into a hall with cream wallpaper and pictures of people. They tried the handle, but the door was locked.

Tad led the way to the back of the house, where there was a smaller porch with some shoes by a doormat. That door was locked, too. He stepped back and looked across the long, sloping lawn to the brick house next door. He thought it would be strange to live so far away from neighbors. In the apartment building where they lived, everyone was close. If you got hurt or sick, you only had to shout and someone would hear you.

They walked around the rest of the house. One high window was open a little. All the rest were closed.

"No one's broken in," said Spugete. "That's something."

"That's nothing," muttered Tad.

"What do you mean—nothing?" Spugete demanded.

Paul stamped his foot. "Stop it, you two!" he said. "I'm going to knock on the front door."

Before they could stop him, he was up the front steps and banging on the door, yelling at the top of his voice, "Miss Barr! Miss Barr! Are you sick, Miss Barr?"

Tad ran after him and grabbed him by the back of the shirt. "Don't be silly!"

Paul pulled away. "If she was hurt or..."

"We'll go and talk to the neighbor," Tad said.

"Which one?" demanded Spugete.

Then they heard Miss Barr inside the house. Her voice seemed muffled and far away. "Help! Help!"

"She's there!" cried Clarene.

"Help! Somebody? Help me!" cried the far-off voice.

"The window! It was open a little bit!" said Tad, and they all ran to the side of the house.

"Miss Barr's okay," Paul said, grinning from ear to ear. "She couldn't yell for help if she was unconscious."

Tad and Clarene looked at each other. Tad said. "You two lift me. If I can get the window off the latch, I'll be able to squeeze through."

They grabbed him around the knees and hoisted him up the wall until he could reach the sill of the small top window. "I think it's the bathroom," he said.

"Put your feet on my shoulders!" called Clarene.

Tad felt her hands guiding his shoes onto her shoulders, and he thought, "Way to go,

Spugete." Now he could easily unhook the window latch, get his arms inside, and pull himself over the sill.

Miss Barr's voice was clearer now. "Is someone there? Help!"

But it seemed to be coming from over Tad's head. He looked up at the bathroom ceiling and then down.

Oh no! Just his luck! The window was right above Miss Barr's toilet, and he was going in head-first. He eased himself down until he could flip the lid over, then he slid the rest of the way down.

He was in. He stood up and called, "Coming, Miss Barr!"

"Who's there?" Her voice was still above his head.

"It's Tad Casey, Miss Barr," he called. "I'm in your bathroom. Where are you?"

"Tad! Thank goodness!" Her voice floated down from above him. "Go into the hall. You'll see the stairs. At the top of the landing there's the door to the attic."

The attic! So that was it. "Are you hurt, Miss Barr?" he called, running up the stairs two at a time.

Her voice was clearer now. "No, Tad, I'm not hurt. But I've been up here since yesterday, and I'm very thirsty!"

"Why didn't you..." He stopped. He saw why. The opening to the attic was far above his head. Lying on the floor was a long stepladder.

Chapter Seven

A Great Team

Miss Barr offered them more lemonade.

"We have to be home before dark," Clarene explained.

"I'll take you in the car," Miss Barr said. "It's the least I can do for my rescuers." She smiled and refilled their glasses. "I didn't know what to do. There are no windows in the attic. I didn't have a rope. No sheets I could tie together. I was getting desperate. I thought I'd have to jump, even if I did risk breaking my legs."

"It's a long way down," Tad said.

"I will definitely have attic stairs put in," said Miss Barr. "A stepladder is too risky. Somehow, I kicked it when I got through the opening. It fell with an awful crash, and there I was, stuck. I didn't even have a cell phone. Have another cookie."

Tad thought that Miss Barr looked normal, apart from the cobwebs in her hair. He took another chocolate cookie and munched while Clarene talked about the day at school.

"So you had Mrs. Isbister!" said Miss Barr. "Oh, she's nice!"

Clarene did her funny eye trick at Tad, rolling them back.

"Very nice," Miss Barr said firmly. "I'll call her tonight and thank her. I'll tell her that three wonderful detectives rescued me, and I'll be at school first thing tomorrow."

"With the spelling test results," thought Tad, but he was too polite to say it.

Paul said, "I was the one who banged on the door and yelled out. Tad and Clarene wanted to go to the neighbor's house."

"I got through the window," Tad said.

"Only because I let you stand on my shoulders," said Clarene.

"I think the three of you make a great team," said Miss Barr. "At school tomorrow, I'll let everyone know that you are my heroes of the year."

She did just that. The next morning at assembly, Miss Barr told the entire school how she'd put some boxes up in her attic. The stepladder had fallen down and she'd been stranded. If Clarene LaValle and Tad and Paul Casey had not come looking for her, why, she could still be there.

"Oo-oo-oo-ooh!" went the entire school.

Then the principal called the Spugete Detectives to the front and shook their hands. "Good job!" he said. "We're very proud of you."

Everyone wanted to talk about the rescue, but it was time for class. Tad and Clarene sat at their desks. They really were heroes. The rest of the class was still watching them.

"I missed you!" said Miss Barr, smiling. "I really missed you all."

"We missed you, too, Miss Barr," Clarene said.

"So let's enjoy this wonderful day together!" Miss Barr reached into her bag for some papers. "First, some scores. Most of you did very well on the spelling test."

Tad sat up straight and folded his arms.

Miss Barr looked at the papers. "The top score went to—Petrov Ulanov!"

What? Tad turned to look at Petrov. That couldn't be right! Petrov came from Russia. He'd only been learning English for four years.

"Well done, Petrov," said Miss Barr. "Now, all of the rainforest projects were good, but there was one student who put in a great deal of time and effort. Her project is amazing."

Tad looked at Clarene, who was wearing her sweet-as-honey smile.

"Diane Baker!" said Miss Barr.

Everyone applauded, and Diane looked like she was going to cry. So did Clarene.

At recess, Tad and Clarene didn't talk much about the spelling test or the rainforest project. Tad *did* go up to Petrov and congratulate him. Petrov merely shrugged his shoulders. "It is not a large deal," he said.

"*Big* deal," corrected Tad.

Petrov nodded. "Exactly," he said.

At lunch, Clarene admitted that Diane Baker's project was better than hers. "I've just seen it," Clarene said. "It's really cool."

Tad said, "I'm glad Petrov got the best grade." Then he frowned. "You know something? I've spoken English all my life. Petrov's spoken it for four years. How can he win a big spelling test, just like that?"

"He works hard," said Clarene. She tucked her arm through his. "At least we're not lonely," she reminded him.

Tad looked at her, then he laughed and laughed. "You're such a Spugete!" he said.